For Mike – M.M.
For my mother – A.K.

This is the Oasis copyright © Frances Lincoln Limited 2005
Text copyright © Miriam Moss 2005
Illustrations copyright © Adrienne Kennaway 2005

The right of Miriam Moss to be identified as the Author,
and of Adrienne Kennaway to be identified as the Illustrator of this Work
has been asserted by them in accordance with the Copyright, Designs and Patents Act, 1988.

First published in Great Britain in 2005 by
Frances Lincoln Children's Books, 4 Torriano Mews,
Torriano Avenue, London NW5 2RZ
www.franceslincoln.com

First paperback edition 2007

British Library Cataloguing in Publication Data available on request

ISBN 978-1-84507-572-9

Printed in Singapore

1 3 5 7 9 8 6 4 2

The Publishers would like to thank Rufus Bellamy and Dena Freeman
for acting as consultants on this book.

This is the
OASIS

Miriam Moss

Illustrated by Adrienne Kennaway

F

FRANCES LINCOLN
CHILDREN'S BOOKS

This is the place, or is it a mirage –
jumping and shimmering
in a hot desert land?

This is the place, the green heart of the desert,
surrounded by mountains
of shape-shifting sand.

This is the place where an old desert monitor
moves through short shadows
with a cool watchful eye.

This is the place where a side-winding viper
shakes scales as a warning,
then slips under hot sand.

This is the place where dust devils, like whirlwinds,
dance spirals of sand dust
high into the air.

This is the place where wind whips up a sandstorm,
which swallows up buildings
and blots out the sun.

This is the place surrounded by date palms
where pools of bright water
spring up from the ground.

This is the place where rivers run silver
into green leafy gardens
of hot peppers and lime.

This is the place where herdsmen lead camels
printing pancake-sized footprints
in long lines in the sand.

This is the place where dry-throated camels
drink gallons of water
in the soft shade of palms.

This is the place where the tall courtly Tuareg,
trade salt, mined in basins,
as precious as gold.

This is the place where people pound millet,
bear children, tend animals
and draw water from wells.

This is the place where raven caws rudely,
and pigeons coo gently
in feathery fronds.

This is the place where visiting swallows
fly feasting on insects
in the cool of the day.

This is the place where millipede trundles
and bright shiny beetles
roll dark balls of dung.

This is the place where hedgehogs hunt nightly
for frogs, fleas and scorpions
and the nest eggs of birds.

This is the place where sand cat and caracal
come creeping and leaping,
both stalking their prey!

This is the place steeped in moonlight and mystery
where the sky streams with bats
under billions of stars.

This is the place where the soft desert daybreak
steals away stars
and melts morning mists.

This is the place that rare rain refreshes,
turning dry desert patches
into meadows of flowers.

This is the place, a green jewel in the desert,
surrounded by mountains of
shape-shifting sand.

This is the oasis.

The Sahara

The Sahara is the world's largest desert. It lies in northern Africa and is about the same size as the United States of America (5150km long and 1610km wide).

The sand dunes in the Sahara can be hundreds of miles long and can reach over 300m high. As well as sand dunes there are plateaux of rock and stone and some snow-capped mountains.

The temperature in the desert soars during the day but plunges at night when it can be so cold that frost forms. The daytime temperature can reach 54.4°C/130°F.

Ancient rock drawings in the middle of the Sahara show that once, thousands of years ago, the Sahara was a green and fertile land where hippos and giraffe lived.

Oases

The word oasis comes from an ancient Egyptian word meaning 'fertile place in the desert'. Three quarters of the Sahara's people live in the hundreds of oases that dot the Sahara. Every oasis has a supply of water, usually a natural spring, at its centre. Date palms grow around the spring, as well as figs, peaches, citrus fruits, wheat and barley. Oases serve as stopping places where desert traders and travellers can stock up on water supplies and food, and share news.

Sandstorms

Strong winds in the Sahara can blow for days on end, kicking up clouds of stinging sand and making it impossible to see more than a few inches. Sometimes these blinding sandstorms bury entire villages under sand. Many of the winds have special names. *Haboob* is the Arab name for a sand-laden wind. *Khamsin* means '50 days', which is how long this wind sweeps across the desert every year. Winter arrives when a strong wind, called the *Harmattan* (which means 'tear your breath apart') arrives and causes temperatures to drop to 15–27°C/60–80°F.

Plants and trees

As it rains only very rarely in the Sahara, many plants survive by having long roots that plunge deep underground to suck water up from under the desert. Other plants only germinate after a heavy rainfall. They grow quickly and bloom, seed and die within a few days. Often their flowers are brightly coloured or very large to attract insects. Desert grasses survive by having roots that can collect water over a very wide area. In hot dry periods the tops wither and only the roots remain alive. Cacti survive in the desert by taking in water when it rains and storing it in their fleshy stems for use in dry spells.

The Tuareg

The Tuareg have lived in the Sahara for thousands of years. They are mainly nomadic, moving their camels, goats, sheep and donkeys from one place to another looking for good pasture land. They always making sure that they are never far from the nearest oasis.

The Tuareg wear striking dyed indigo robes. The loose-fitting layers of cotton protect them from the harsh desert sun and keep them cool by trapping moisture. The ceremonial turban worn by men is called the *tagelmust*.

Tuareg music, poetry and song are passed down from generation to generation by the women who teach their children to read and write, sing songs, dance and play music.

Trading Salt

Many Tuareg trade in salt mined from deep in the Sahara. Long ago the oceans that covered the Sahara dried up, leaving salt behind. In places rich with salt, holes are dug and filled with water. When the water dries away in the sun, the salt crystals left are collected and moulded into salt cakes. These are wrapped in palm-fibre mats before being loaded on to camels. Camel caravans, which can be up to a mile long, bring the precious salt back to the Sahara's edge to be sold.

Camels

Camels are perfectly suited to the desert's harsh climate. They don't actually store water in their humps as many people believe. Their humps are made of fatty tissue from which the camels draw energy when food is scarce. Camels store water in their bloodstream and can go without drinking for over a week. When they do find water they can drink up to 40 gallons at a time!

MORE TITLES FROM
FRANCES LINCOLN CHILDREN'S BOOKS

This is the Tree
Miriam Moss
Illustrated by Adrienne Kennaway

The ancient and extraordinary baobab tree takes centre stage
in this poetic and informative story of the wildlife of Africa.
Old as a volcano, the 'upside-down' tree plays a vital role
in the lives of all the creatures which feed on its leaves,
doze in its shade or nest in its branches.

ISBN 978-0-7112-1491-0

This is the Reef
Miriam Moss
Illustrated by Adrienne Kennaway

Follow sharks, turtles and swirling shoals of fish in an extraordinary
and inspiring journey through the Great Barrier Reef.
This is a celebration of a unique and fragile eco-system
and the marine life it feeds, shelters and protects.

ISBN 978-1-84507-573-6

Jungle Song
Miriam Moss
Illustrated by Adrienne Kennaway

When Little Tapir is woken by Spider and led deep into the jungle,
he meets all sorts of wildlife, who add their own rhythms to the wild song.
But when the beat stops and Little Tapir is all alone, he realises
just how dangerous the jungle song can be!

ISBN 978-1-84507-428-9

Frances Lincoln titles are available from all good bookshops.
You can also buy books and find out more about your favourite titles,
authors and illustrators on our website: www.franceslincoln.com